SCARRY WORD BOO
On Holiday

Illustrated by Richard Scarry

Hamlyn
London · New York · Sydney · Toronto

Holiday Time

Holiday time is here.
Everybody is going on holiday.
Some go by train, some go by car, some take a ferry across the river.
Do you see Squeaky Mouse?
He is going by raft.

Point to:

railway line
railway crossing
train
car
raft
ferry

5

Happy Flying!

Cat is going away for his holiday.
He is going in a big aeroplane.
Look! Penny Pig has her own aeroplane.

Can you see?

big aeroplane
Penny Pig's aeroplane
pilot
tail
wing
wheel
propeller
suitcases

In the Mountains

Have you ever been to the mountains?
You can play in the woods or wade in a mountain stream.
Do you see some climbers on a cliff?
Look out!
Something is falling.
Can you see what it is?

Point to:

log cabin
axe
pine trees
rope
climbers
cliff

At the Lake

Look at all the boats sailing on the lake!
The wind makes the sailing boat go.
A motor makes the motorboat go.
Do you know what makes the rowing boat go?

Point to:

houseboat
speedboat
fishing boat
sailing boat
motorboat

On the Beach

The Rabbits are spending their holiday at the seaside.

Can you see?

beach chair sand castle sun
steps seagull lifeguard
seashell bathing hut hats
umbrella spade flags

Camping

The Foxes are on a camping trip.
They have set up their tent, table, and bed.
Mr Fox is cooking supper on the barbecue.
Later they will both go to sleep in their tent.
Do you see some ants coming for supper?
Do you think the Foxes will be happy to see them?

Point to:

mustard	ants	barbecue
hot dog	tent	picnic basket
car	bed	table

Special Days

Kitty's birthday is during the summer holiday.
Can you see Kitty's birthday cake?
How old is Kitty today?
Easter is a holiday.
Then we see lots of chicks and bunnies and Easter eggs.

Christmas is the best holiday of all.
Christmas is not a holiday for Father Christmas though.
He goes to work, bringing presents to children everywhere.

Find these on the tree:

house   red ball
bird   striped ball
angel   blue ball

Winter Holiday

It is cold in the winter.
Sometimes there is
lots of ice and snow.
Can you see
somebody skiing?
How many rabbits are
riding on a toboggan?
Who has a red
sledge?
Squeaky is throwing a
snowball at Bear.
Bear is playing a
game called ice
hockey.

Raccoon has made a hole in the ice and is
fishing through it.
Do you think she will catch anything?

Point to:

skis
hockey stick
toboggan
ice skates
sledge
snowball

Staying at Home

Bear is staying at home this holiday.
But he is not lonely.
Some of his friends are staying at home, too.

Bear's friends, the kitten sisters, are playing ring-a-ring-o'-roses.
They like the part where they all fall down best.

Things to do at home

fly paper aeroplanes
play ring-a-ring-o'-roses
have a tea party
play with a ball
help with the washing
go for a walk

More things to do at home

Play a game with a friend.
Bear has the black pieces and Rabbit has the red ones.
Bear is thinking hard, but Rabbit is winning.